BRADFORD C. CHASE

CODBONES

PAUL CORDEIRO, EDITOR

wrinkled sea press

Codbones

Copyright © Bradford C. Chase

Editor: Paul Cordeiro

All rights reserved. Printed in the United States of America. No part of this book may be used or reproduced in any manner whatsoever without written permission except in the case of reprints in the context of reviews.

Wrinkled Sea Press
P.O. Box 234
S. Orleans, Massachusetts 02662
www.wrinkledsea.com
info@wrinkledsea.com

ISBN 978-1-7377477-2-7

Back cover photo of Brad Chase by Shane MacNeill
All other photos by Brad Chase

Text and cover design by Charita Patamikakorn

ACKNOWLEDGEMENTS

The author expresses gratitude and appreciation to Gerry Grenier of Wrinkled Sea Press for taking a chance on Codbones *and giving guidance and a forum for poets outside of published circles. Sincere thanks are sent out the editor, Paul Cordeiro, for shaping up this collection as part of his generous mentoring on the world of poetry at various downtown New Bedford venues. And there is no one explainable reason why poets put words together. Inspiration from loss, love, nature and family are always near. With that, I am humbled and blessed by the support, experience and love that flows like the tide from friends and family.*

POEMS

NEPTUNE'S PRIDE — 3
BEMO LEDGE — 4
SUNTORY — 7
VIGO — 9
JOSEFINA — 11
GATEWAY — 13
HIGHLANDS — 15
LEDGEMONT — 17
BROCK AVENUE — 19
CINNAMON BAY — 21
SIREN CALL — 22
EMMA — 24
RETURN AS SPIRITS — 26
THE FRONT — 31
EXIT — 33
DRIFTING SHADOWS — 35
FIRST PARISH — 37
HERMIT — 39
RING THE BELL — 41
BACKSTREET — 43
SUPERMARKET — 44
WHITE LIGHT — 46
SIX WEEKS — 48
HOWARD STREET — 50
NOHOCH MUL — 52

55 — SUBTERRANEAN
56 — RUNAWAY TRAIN
58 — CHARLIE
61 — MIGRATION
65 — IMPOSSIBLE LOVE
67 — IF THIS IS LOVE
69 — SWEET ANGEL FALLING
71 — ELAINE MARIE
73 — TWIN WILLOWS
75 — WINTER'S DREAM
76 — RED DRESS
78 — LOW LIGHT
80 — CAT ISLAND
83 — SHE CALLS
85 — MAGICAL
86 — ONLY ONE
89 — DUNES OF MONOMOY
91 — DONNA B.
93 — SAMUEL JOSEPH
95 — BOOM BOOM BENJAMIN
97 — GRACE
99 — GALLOWAY
100 — MIDDLE BORN
103 — HAWKSNEST

NEPTUNE'S PRIDE

Calmness of the ocean
Born with the change of tide
Eases pain of motion
Dead man's labor washed aside

Cracks in the seaside boulders
Have seen it all before
No man-made stock is older
Forgotten creatures frozen in the core
Life cycles that the sea sustain
Blend in stark synchronicity
No waste is made without gain
Death is in accord with necessity

If the passing of 200 years
Brings change to the path of the moon

What consequence will this have
Upon the diurnal swoon?

Such questions will not confront our wise
Whose efforts went not to peace

Neptune's pride will have reclaimed
The ocean floor we lease

There will be no one to say a prayer
For fields no longer plowed

Tides can prove no beauty
To a restless nuclear cloud

GLOUCESTER, MA

BEMO LEDGE

I hit Bemo Ledge at sixteen knots
Hit old Bemo in the fog
Not too smart but I ain't dead
Cold water is all around
With warm blood on my head

Never saw the breakers before we hit
Running hard in fog for no good reason
Just two totes of codfish onboard
Now I'm in the rollers and all busted up
Trying to keep my body off the ledge

A month from now I'd be done from the chill
If I keep moving, I have a chance
I can't see a thing
I can hear the surf at Brace Cove
Telling me where I need to go

I remember when Stevie hit Salvages
With his dragger one December night
Those boys were asleep in their bunks
As the Northeast wind blew
And the ocean rushed in

It's the Captain that plots the course
And it's the crew that takes it on the chin
No bigger fool for what I did
Hands on the wheel, pushing through fog
But a lucky fool can stay alive
Not much else for me to do

My wife left me two years before
And my boys won't see me now
The Sheila B. meant everything to me
Now she belongs to Bemo Ledge

I hit Bemo Ledge at sixteen knots
Hit old Bemo in the fog
Not too smart but I ain't dead
I hit Bemo Ledge at sixteen knots

Some set a course in life
But never follow
Some set the wrong course
But never know
I've been 10 degrees off my whole life
Running that line hard into these rocks

I hit Bemo Ledge at sixteen knots
Hit old Bemo in the fog
Not too smart but I ain't dead
I hit Bemo Ledge at sixteen knots

GLOUCESTER, MA

SUNTORY

Five thousand miles from my home
Whiskey glass within my reach
Can't call nobody on the telephone
Can't meet my friend at the beach

What about love on this ocean?
Is it hidden as a clam holds a pearl?
Maybe whiskey is the right potion
That guy says he'll be my girl

Up from misery, down to shame
With the waves my emotions roll
I substitute work for this pain
My blues are under control

As the sun falls from the sky
I swear the water seems black
Without this tear in my eye
It's really the darkest of blue

So give me that glass of Suntory
Maybe time won't pass by so slow
I'll tell you a made-up story
Seeing there ain't no place to go

When there's no love to be gained
There's no reason for love lost
It's best to set my mind out for a stroll
I'll think better of lonely oceans crossed
My blues are under control

F/V KUMANO MARU, BERING SEA

VIGO

The mighty swell if frozen still
Would seem a hill of finely chiseled metallic hues
Fanatic wind and wave fast erode this ever-changing sight
Gale spikes rip through the crest, spuming white
Leaving a wound of icy, aqua blue

F/V VIGO, ATLANTIC OCEAN

JOSEFINA

Josefina, Josefina, *mucho mal tiempo*
I cannot see you
You are many miles from here
I can feel your anger
Your anger moves the air

So young and full of life
Which way will you turn?
Last night I could not sleep
Lost in deep concern
Watching in mute wonder
As waves tempt me from the rail
I guess that I will join you
If my vessel should fail

Josefina, Josefina, *chica peligrosa*
You don't need to find land
If you met del Golfo your raging may cease
You'll find him warm and persuasive
And go make love toward the East

F/V CHICHA TOUZA, ATLANTIC OCEAN

GATEWAY

From across the deep there is no choice
But to watch unfold the daily harvest
Ripe for one moment are the tinted wisps
That great painters could never come to use
It seems a gateway of tapered flame
Gentle seas of azure rise from the fire's golden hues

The evolving scene is so enchanting
I fear that next I'll see
The flight of cherubic angels descending
Through streams of mellow lightning and pools of thunder
Gracious in proving me to be mistaken
Demanding no more than humble wonder

The shapes and colors captivate my gaze
With subtle change they remain
After the majestic beacon leaves without a whisper
She steals away for strange lands to roam
This must be the gateway to the West
That beckons me forth to my home

F/V EGUNSENTIA, ATLANTIC OCEAN

HIGHLANDS

Purple sand and goldenrods
Pitch pines wink at driftwood logs
Beyond the surf finbacks blow
Grey clay weeps at the Highland's toe

This temple will not last forever
Gremlins of wind, rising sea and gravity
Will bring a balance
Destruction or resurrection?
The elements are the same
As before glaciers raised these holy lands

Endless schools of pogies unmolested
Choices never made nor protested
This culture is not yours to change
No fish within casting range

The pines and scrub oaks
Tumble along the slope
Truncated in size and life
Roots clinging to the crest
We are the same
A correction is due

Irrigation pipes and septic tanks
Slide down the sacrificial banks
Shadows creep on the heavy shore
Grey seals take a chance in the Backside's roar

HARWICH, MA

LEDGEMONT

Four inches of rain fell on Portuguese Hill
It came quickly in the early hours
Following a front of crackling light and rumbling gods
The streets flowed like a river as the sun cut through the last of it

The view from Ledgemont could come from a dream
The air and water are still
Not a wake for miles
The last trace of fog clings to the breakwater

The Lady of Good Voyage bells rejoice the cleansing
The dark stones of St. Ann's are silent
No one is outside yet
The streets have been washed clean of everything
The sins of the father, injustice and desperation
Have been swept offshore with the squall

For the moment, the glory of this fabled port rises in the light air
The flooding tide, the shining granite and the angel of Green Street
All wink and smile at these sturdy homes that watch over the harbor
Holding the hopes and dreams of a better day

GLOUCESTER, MA

BROCK AVENUE

Running between East and West Beaches
Past the faded clapboard tripledeckers
The stoops and porches that keep time
The quiet spaces of Hazelwood Park
Is the South End's artery and universe
The university of Brock Avenue

The craggy Sycamores are the elders
Leaning in to compete for sunlight
Stout, but not so tall
Irreverent, chaotic branches
That throw shade with leaves
And wild shadows without

The salted breeze rises
With the morning sun
Shining down on the Avenue
Flaring northwest to greet the City
Generations walked to the mills
To Berkshire-Hathaway, Potomska, and Kilburn
With lunch boxes and coffee mugs
Made to last a lifetime
These memories slowly fade
As a new crew greets the changing day

NEW BEDFORD, MA

CINNAMON BAY

The sea is coming up
With a pace and resolve
That people can barely detect
The clock of our lifetime
Has no role in this
The rise transcends generations and race
We are within this tide and the cause

You can hope for a reversal
Or accept the pause that is your time
Or rail with worry and indignation
With all the determination
Of the tiny plankton washing on the beach
To fire bright green on a moonless night
Free of any expectation
Until the ebb has left you on a shoal
To expire in a furious chemical reaction
Or swept randomly out to freedom
To live another day

Species of this planet
Will ebb and flood with no more influence
Than the plankton on the sand
Only humans who leap and fall
Outside the laws of survival
Have the will to back off the beach
Burning green into the night

ST. JOHN, USVI

SIREN CALL

For a moment everything seems normal
Her smile is meant for me alone
Yet she cannot shelter herself
From the light that enters the window
The glare from outside changes her face
She's become a child that rules half of the world
I sink into the floor
As she speaks in clear tones
A deep breath rushes out of the room

"Can you smell the blood, mon cheri?
You know it's so hard to drink alone
We've lost the fear of being eaten alive
So go where the feast is more than fuel
I'll remain to rave with archangels
When you are ready to return to my side
You'll have no control of your passage
As we meet at the turn of the tide"

She backs away from the door
blending into the light
My body becomes a mass of slow-moving lead
I fall through a black, moonless night
Coming to rest in a swamp I know well
Darkness deletes all sense of sight
Senses of smell and sound are nourished by fright
I hear the wind and moan of a forgotten bell buoy
The bell has long rusted still
While the whistle stays true
In memory of those lost on the shoals
The mist from the sea
Entrances me with the scent of salt and iodine weed

I tumble to my knees in wet sand
As the wind whispers then roars
To excite the rush of incoming breakers
Each wave seems a life of its own
I fear that the sounds that I hear
Are of more than wind and waves
Instantly, I prepare for what I could never believe

The spirits come freely out of the swells
Striding through the surf gracefully
I beg them to share their experience
The language they speak has no meaning to me
Shining eyes roll in response to my screams

The clothes they have I cannot wear
The indifference they possess I cannot share
Peacefully, they settle into the dunes
At my feet comes the hiss
Of the cold dying kiss
As the last pulse of each wave touches the shore

I awake in the sand to the warmth of the sun
And the siren call of her voice
Asking so softly, "What was the sin of Lucifer?
Was he simply tired of paradise?"
The sky is blue and boundless
The shore slopes with perfection to a calm sea
My body is as limber as a jungle cat
My blood boils with the luster of mercury

I begin to move along the beach
Oh, so vacantly
Towards a dream that is quite out of reach
By the reef I will wait
Oh, so patiently
For the dead man to wash up on the beach

HARWICH, MA

EMMA

I hear you coughing, brother
We both know what is going on
You better than I
The slow march of cells failing
As subtle as a chuckle at first
Now a telltale morning rumble
Is it the innocent whine of a fan belt
Or the steady scouring of tired pistons?

They sold you smokes for a good price
A captive market for eight months at sea
They gave you cardboard to sleep on
Treating crew like cattle
While you spoke seven languages
With confidence that found comfort
In ports of call from the Ivory Coast
To Amsterdam, to Lisbon, and Salem

I see you on the stoop, brother
Watching the world in just that moment
Not saying much until asked
A soft hello to every passerby
That blazing smile before kind words
To lift the day for that one person
More instinct than congeniality
As warm and lush as honey in tea

I see you smiling, my brother
I cannot imagine a consciousness
That has seen dreams come and go
Felt the loss of love across oceans
Held sadness with no chance to grieve
Rose up the steep wave of random passion
To find no one calling in the twilight
Yet a smile is there for all
That life itself cannot extinguish

HARWICH, MA

RETURN AS SPIRITS

We used to be friends
We'd shock each other on the telephone
I swear sometimes you'd read my mind
I'd enrage you with a change of tone
Once a weakness lay down the bricks
Supple ivy began to grow
Faced with stubborn mortar
It was easiest to let it go

One day we laughed at broken windows
The next we lied of breaking hearts
Nothing stopped, no doors were closed
Ambition carved us worlds apart
And if we were to meet once more
Why should I not feel like I did before?

To think of you brings different pain
It settles now, blending unsure sentiment
Turning blue to gray like summer rain
Flowing forever out, this tide is spent
Suppose death does move free of shame
I used to know what that word meant

Oh Annabelle, I miss you the most
Do you ever think of me?
The crest of sleep is guarded by your ghost
The smell of your hair is brought by the sea
The same sea that swept you from my coast
Leaving my love a tattered sail, forever in a lee

We used to be friends
After school, in a swamp, down the road, at a beach
Changing fears, gaining ego, stirred dreams, spurned time
In a gym, on a ship, at an island out of reach
A wound that bleeds, while another heals
All these faces have gone free
Yet return as spirits to my sleep
Dear memory, you swell virtue with vanity
But cannot bring back these friends to me

F/V WILLI BREDEL, ATLANTIC OCEAN

THE FRONT

Reason falters
Restores the mind to ancient altars
Emotions climax
Nerves coiled for attack
Rockets in the distance
Bring terrified resistance
You and I must try
While we still can

Desires increase
Only death will bring peace

ST. THOMAS, USVI

EXIT

Old man took a stroll today
He did so in a peculiar way
Leaving his boots and body home to stay
The old man died, that is to say

As he left, he had a thought
Of the used book he just bought
Over if it was his or not
Too late man, it is time to rot

He returns to a realm
From where he came
If he was never here
All would be the same

He'll walk alone
Destination unknown
To a boy who grew
From the union of two

HARWICH, MA

DRIFTING SHADOWS

The same concrete walls
Cobwebs and cracked floors
Steel bars and drifting shadows
Days go by without expectation of freedom
Was I born in this prison cell?
Or did I earn this debt?
Incarcerated in a tomb
That is my own mind

Sometimes I wake in peace
A mere ripple moving across a pond
Then the ticking clock accelerates
What have I done?
To bring such disconnect
From my waking intentions
With the tangled web of thoughts
To the eyes of those I meet
And the words that leave my mouth

Oh lord, I'd do anything
To take this lead off my chest
Rise up off my knees
Let gravity calm the ripples
For more than a few moments
On the rare day when
A stranger's smile greets me
Crows call out from the trees
And the sun shines all day

HARWICH, MA

FIRST PARISH

Why no dry eyes?
For the faithless at the funeral
As tempting as the widow's veil
Are the glorious myths of salvation,
Immaculate guidance and a reunion in the sky
Our molecules are only borrowed
Saints are recycled the same as sinners

The stained glass and sculpted oak
Raise respect for those who built this temple
Giving in grace so long ago
Comfort radiates from the rafters in the preacher's pause
Is this sadness slyly transposed?
From the wreckage of our own lives
Or cumulative, facing the weight of death?

A simple man praised at the altar
For kindness, altruism, and laughter
And love for a random soul
That at one time
Stopped the earth from turning
The faithless weep at this ritual
Knowing a hard end has come

HARWICH, MA

HERMIT

Waiting for tomorrow
Hung up in the brambles
Picking up pennies
Throwing out nickels

Waiting for an angel
Tightrope fettered faithful
Drawn to the serpent's rattle
Did you hear the statute prattle?

Waiting for the shark bite
Hitherto impulsive but polite
Necropolis graced by moonlight
Iodine keeps me upright

Waiting for your ghost
Wanting that the most
Drifting at the cloud line
Comfortable in quicklime

Waiting for rigor mortis
Molecules from a tortoise
Conceived in meteorites
Settling in the forest

HARWICH, MA

RING THE BELL

Is it wrong to recycle?
The topical verse of a bard?

I did read them all
Every word carefully
Thinking of who you might be
Looking for lyrics among one-liners
And fingerprints of the muse

It is fine
To let go of most
Keeping only the finest
After all
The words were written
For the writer
To mark their time
Waiting by the freeway
For that rare, ecstatic jewel
To ring the bell
Defy the setting sun
Bleeding heaven into hell

HARWICH, MA

BACKSTREET

The smell of dusty gray cement
A path of uneven sidewalk
Cracked over restless years
The sound of a cricket's lonely itch
Calling too soon for a change of season
The oak keeps time with a gentle sway
A fog whistle saddened by the offset rhythm
Both charmed by the southwest breeze

    All these images move me

From stubborn thought and swollen daydream
Only for a few spellbound moments
Which is enough
To part the stream of central themes
Leaving behind the hours squandered
When worthy concepts become crowded
By recurring visions of heroic romance
And the blurring of reality with obsession

I wonder how many years will pass
Till a day goes by when I don't think of you
Will my next love be as strange as the last?
Or lurch like a misfit from out of the blue?

NARRAGANSETT, RI

SUPERMARKET

Going down to Wal-Mart
To think about life for awhile
Looking for a good deal and moral tokens
Checking out those precocious teens
Gonna buy a beef stick
For forty-nine cents
Gonna watch the beefcakes
Buying plastic fence

Going down to Wal-Mart, Baby
You can't come along
I've got to do this by myself
Can't separate right from wrong
I hear they got a special on dirt
At a buck-fifty a bag
They took out a meadow on a 10-cent margin
Adding nasty chemicals
To mix with our yards and blood

Is this the reason?
The Pilgrims dumped the King
Is this the reason?
The Berlin Wall came down
This is the reason
That dude stole the rubber seed

Going down to Wal-Mart
For maybe one more century
Locking in a consumer base
China's Cheshire grin
Making money off mass extinction
My cart is filling up
With useless technology,
Cancer fuel, and trinkets of cultural delight

SHREWSBURY, MA

WHITE LIGHT

When the white light burns too brightly
I'll move myself down the street
To where lovers meet
And the lonely find seats
Where I can clutch a brown bottle tightly

The mirror becomes alive with reflections
Blurred by smoke and bar bottle glow
The women I see flourish in this light
Their eyes graced with the gravity they hold
The man to my right has departed in flight
To a place that makes his face fold
A young man laughs in the face of rejection
I watch the shine on my face grow

The night passes nearly in silence
Peering at times from side to side
I avoid looking up as the view is enchanting
From my image there is no place to hide
My mind is blushing with endless fancy
The sweat from my legs has me stuck to the seat
Seems I only forget when I'm up dancing
Thanks, Johnny, I'm too tight to move my feet

A bottle of rye
To drink til I die
The plaster and I
Are in accord
White without sun
Coming undone
Bow traddle doe, dee traddle dum
Wait, is she looking at me?

Well then, I'm looking at you
To you I raise my glass high and proud
Somehow, I miss my mouth
Still the liquid spills out
My darling turns toward the crowd
Laughing out loud
I return to my shroud

Soon the bartender says:
"Unless there is someone you're waiting to see
it looks like to me
that maybe it's time you should go"
And I say, "Yes, thank you, you're quite right
I've been waiting for more than one night
Please have patience and this person will show
Put your whiskey in my glass
it will help my time pass,
you see, I'm waiting for someone I don't know"

SALEM, MA

SIX WEEKS

I'm too tight
I'm way too tight tonight
Sitting here thinking
What it would be like
To move through a crowd
Raise my voice up loud
And still feel alright
Yeah, I'm too tight

I'm not sure when this fog descended
To burden my reason with spite
To anchor my feet by this windowsill
Waiting for darkness to domineer the light
Must try not to impose this condition
On the people I know
Or the ones passing by on the street
To the new ones I meet
I can hardly speak
While my eyes ramble through a tour
That their eyes never asked for
I pursue only those who offer rejection
I adore the one holding the noose
From the ones that are loving
I run out of sight
The running feels like freedom
That should keep my body loose
Yet, I wait up alone
The very next night
For a ghost that knows better
Than to return to be haunted
Where there is no afterlife

I don't find inspiration in society
And the comfort of grain is deceiving
With a few bottles down
I swell with such pride
That the smile of a stranger
Can take me so high
Only to reach the edge, and slip over
And the joy I molded turns to clay
A brittle enclosure that holds only dense fluids
What spills out is unfit for public display
An hour ago, I laughed with prized eyes
Now, I resent the long-coat dandies
With more money than Jesus
And the punchy drunk dustbowls
Proud of their puke
And the flowing sweet Debbies
Knowing and strong as the tides
One look and they know I am way gone
With nothing they value to hide

Maybe I'll stretch myself out on the boardwalk
Soaking up the infra-red sights
That ease from the shadows
Sending off brilliant moods of love and life
Deflecting my focus to remain cool and polite
My gaze and gait lock firmly ahead
Stumbling between the past and present
All the while, endlessly thinking to myself
What it would be like
To touch, to taste, to feel

If only I wasn't so tight tonight

SALEM, MA

HOWARD STREET

On a street with homes on one side only
It's a cold night to be dead in the ground
On one side there is life
Through windows fogged from the heat
White light and pale shadows are found
Bright colored houses have turned toward each other
Looking away from a prosperous town
The wind whips without mercy on the other side
Where ice and rust have the gate frozen as still
As the memory of those laid down
The stones that keep time
Are as cold as the air
Rising up through the snow
That covers the names of those lying below

The radio says we should stay in our beds
For the wind can stop your heart cold
To the ones with no homes
And the ones who've grown old
Seek shelter and keep yourself warm
To the ones in the ground
Lay still without a sound
The cold is just fine
For the hundred years before
And the next thousand more

To dream of your death is nothing to fear
If in waking your dreams are alive
Live each day as if your last
Rejoice with each year passed
That you haven't claimed your rightful place underground

It is a comfort to know
You'll go no place else
And the grass will grow green in the spring
Your love will live within me
Until my time ends
As the stones above crumble to dust
And the bones below feed the earth

I'll walk past here fast
Looking over my shoulder
Adoring the cold wind on my face
The shining ice on the street
Is heaven enough for my feet
On either side there is no resting place.

SALEM, MA

NOHOCH MUL

What ancient souls remain?
Is there only dust?
Once earth, once proud
The vines and roots were cleared from the steps
Yet overrun the other sides
One hundred steps above the jungle
How many years, how many eyes?

The trees below move like ocean waves
Countless currents form and cease
Outside the bounds of time
The peak is the pathway of the hawk
That soars in search of prey
The view alone sanctified their quest
Rousing flight in human dreams

What society could summon the sweat and vision?
To place these stones to such a height
Was it built to please their gods?
Out of thanks for life and food to eat
Or was it built to honor one man
On the backs of those born low
Like so many temples that still stand

Oh, the arch of history
How easily it bends
Marauder, damn your judgements
Were these ruins once paradise?
Does one species control the pulse of destiny?
This clan will never know
The slaves are gone
Another faith has been imposed

The hawk was here before these stones
Passing the torch with each prey found
With the grace of wind will retain this height
To watch them crumble to the ground

COBA, MEXICO

SUBTERRANEAN

Subconscious, subterranean
Faith and reason
Intracellular, supernatural
Some believe very strongly
The soul takes these into consideration
Although it doesn't need to
And can dismiss them
With the grace of the lord above

Sometimes I think my soul is in my penis
Resolutely forging passion
Ripping the reason in my mind asunder
Divine enough; not so ever lasting
Soon it goes to other places

If you want my soul
Now, you can find it
Down, deep in the water
Laughing loudly
It's very moody
Can't be taken seriously
Like the weather
It can change in a heartbeat
Watch the shining prism turn to gray

When you die
It is like a light switch
That you shut off
Only darkness
And it won't come on again

SALEM, MA

RUNAWAY TRAIN

This rack of bones is a runaway train
Ridden by hobo thoughts that hitch and hop
Then tumble free into the weeds
To sleep in the rain
Never to see where the train comes to stop

These bums they light fires
Kindled with busted oak boxes
To keep themselves warm
And alight the dark patches of ground
Where they dwell temporarily
On cool, dank nights the wood smolders
Throwing smoke that discourages bugs
While shedding little light

On clear moonlit nights the fire blazes
Setting the ground sparkling with the glint
Of cracked coal and broken booze bottles
On such nights, these bums get along
There is enough wine and food for all
They are at peace, in good company
Stretching on the ground like cats
There is nothing they need
Until morning

The train whistle screams
The bums bound to their feet
With no reason to leave
There is no reason to stay
Running like mad
They pile into the first open boxcar
Laughing at their good fortune

To have the morning sun shining in
On a free ride to who knows where
All openly agree that this is the life
Spirits of the muse rise from oil-soaked pallets
Twirling in a jig to the clapping of hands
And screeching of dry pistons
The meekest of bums sprouts horns
The blackest of hearts melts under a halo
Time is relaxed as the train levitates
Sparks fly as wheels fight to remain on the tracks
A family of cannibals
Furiously trading chatter and insults
All inwardly wonder if the rhythm is random
Each silently bearing the toll

Take a chance – take a drink
Gotta be crazy – think too much
What about me? – what will I do?
Got no chicken – eat a cracker

SALEM, MA

CHARLIE

Charlie went crazy
He told me yesterday
Charlie went crazy
He didn't look that bad to me
Maybe a little nervous
Wide-eyed nervous
I said, "where you been, man?"
"They sent me to the funny farm
To play cards with the fruit cakes
I started hearing voices
Very strange voices
Got scared of young kids
Couldn't talk to strangers
Told my wife I'm going crazy
She laughed right at me
And kept on watching TV
While scratching poison ivy"

"One day, everything was accelerating
I was hyper like an insect
Spent the day curled up
Focused on ceramic tiles
My wife says, "you on something, Charlie?"
I said, "yeah, the bathroom floor
That trick bought me a ticket
To three weeks of observation"
"So, you really went nuts?"
"Oh yeah, I'm feeling better now
Got me on medication
Working on my confidence
Everybody needs a reservoir of satisfaction

Gonna build a power base
Consolidating budget and squeezing payroll
To relax, I've been drinking myself silly
While surfing the web"

Well, you never know
Who's going to go crazy
Charlie went crazy
He told me yesterday

SALEM, MA

MIGRATION

The boy walks out into the grey rain
His sullen boredom conjures myths of pain
Mother wonders why he lingers in the wet
Her thoughts spin to images she cannot forget

A black duck with a orange bill
I've never seen a duck like that before
It has seen me many times
It knows my pulse, the way I move
With due regard, it slowly swims away
The rain wets my jeans
Until cloth presses tight against skin
A sudden chill. A change in store

The wind and sea conspire
To shape the curve of the coast
A vibrant stream cut from tidal surge
No creatures mourn and fall in fear
Beach grass embrace the lack of flow
Expanding their reign with each absent tide
There is nothing that they need to know
They simply grow. I'm out of here

Refreshed, soaked to the bone, he returns inside
Beaming, her love responds to wet clothes on the rack
Dispelled are fears of dark discontent.
"Oh, you've come back!"
Yes, but only for a moment

NARRAGANSETT, RI

IMPOSSIBLE LOVE

I saw her the other night
At a fire on the beach
I wished to take her home
Our eyes met for a moment of bliss
Was her smile for me alone?
No, it was as distant as her kiss

She knows who I am
At least knows my face
The look in my eyes
The t-shirts that I wear
Is this relief to realize?
I really don't have a prayer

How would it feel?
To awake next to her Madonna eyes
The scent of her hair
Upon my pillow
This is something
I will never know

HARWICH, MA

IF THIS IS LOVE

She comes on so playfully
Knows how things ought to be
I did not choose her prophecy
This is all new to me
If this is love, take it away

The one I want is a mystery
She's hot and cold, oh so free
Precious dreams across the sea
Perhaps it's just my company
If this is love, take it away

Cast into her daydream plans
While my thoughts are saved for one
I turn a friend away
Disconnected, I don't stay
Another port, another freeway
Hurdling over the memories

Is this finally the end?
Never to be the same
When she leaves, I know
Summer has come and gone

I can lounge with a lie
I could drink til I die
She won't move from my mind
It only hurts when I try
If this is love, take it away

HARWICH, MA

SWEET ANGEL FALLING

Lost flame
Her thoughts are sinking
Forever tame
The endless thinking
No words to share
In early morning
No answered prayers
Sweet angel falling
Love was tender
Love is over
Love best forgotten
Love is never

HARWICH, MA

ELAINE MARIE

Do you really love her?
Or is she just a substitute?
I don't believe you need her
You only want to possess
Her body of flesh
As a shrine for your caress
You cannot have her

No, I swear it's not that way
She's unlike anyone I've ever known
Without her love, I'd never stay
The confidence of her hopes and fears
Is all I wish to hold
And when we start loving
I will only think of you
If only her man would go away
You'd see a change in me today
You cannot have her
Yes, I know

Elaine Marie, you will never know
The wealth of love in this heart I hold

Elaine Marie, you will never see
The shine of a world where you are with me

Elaine Marie, you will never feel
The breathless passion I am forced to conceal

Elaine Marie, will you ever set free?
A soul drowning in love that can never be

SALEM, MA

TWIN WILLOWS

Cars assault the rain-soaked pavement beyond the window
Immersed in her bed-borne warmth and hissing wetness,
I slide toward sleep
I wake to white walls
And the same whistling protest from the avenue
My ankles hang cool over the end of the bed
My body clings to the edge as she slumbers in the middle

With window up and no curtain there
The light and noise flush my mind awake
I remember the pints we drank, Her pants as we danced
We argued over the limits of reason compared to belief
We fought like sexless jackals in the early morning
I pushed you to the ground outside the bar
Hiding my face as I pressed against you
To shade the sadness sweeping upward

It's alright to feel this way
She is too free to be kept
And I don't love her too much yet
You go so long, and everything is fine
Suddenly it's no good

I know now I am leaving soon
The rush of every car compounds my guilt
The sound of motion steals my breath away
And reaffirms my faith in knowing
I'd be the bigger fool to stay

NARRAGANSETT, RI

WINTER'S DREAM

When I woke this morning
We were still in love
Until I saw that same old wall
Until I saw that same old wall
The sky was blue and you were with me
Wind swept marsh grass rolled beneath our feet
You never told me why you went away
You didn't mention why you went away
How can love last a lifetime?
When you still love me in my sleep
Lust set to blaze by the August moon
Never burns through the smoke of a winter's dream
What if they knew I was thinking of you?
Yes, it's true I only think of you
What if we were to meet again?
I wonder what I'd do
I believe it would tear me apart
Yes, I'm sure it would tear me apart
What if you were to say hello
Like you use to do?
Don't want to spend my life in a bar
Don't want to spend my life in a bar
Along I go, never to know, right at the bar

SALEM, MA

RED DRESS

She's good business
When the band's in town
Single guys drink faster
And always stick around
She's a conductor of the blues
Other women do the best they can
Keeping one eye on her
And the other on their man
Red Dress!
She's got a red dress on

A virtuoso of motion
She works the beat real slow
Hands on her waist, knees bent
Slowly rocking as the clock ticks six times
When the bass line swings
Her heels come together
As she dips to the floor
It's the kind of move
That the whole room sees
It's the kind of move
Makes a grown man believe
All the wonders of nature
That pull tides through the seas
That push winds through the trees
That bring prophets to their knees
Grow cold in the shadow
Of her back-step sway

Red dress!
She got a red dress on

When the chorus lead rips
Her shoulders move side-to-side
One red strap slips
As her arms go up high
Her right leg steps back
The other starts to slide
Your skull is going crack
When her hips join the ride

What are you going to do tomorrow?
Think about her red dress
Red dress!
Everybody knows
She got a red dress on

GLOUCESTER, MA

LOW LIGHT

I know you can find yourself a lover
In any dive in this city
You're a queen of the low light
In a one-piece, green mini skirt
Carving up the bar room
As you rumble to your seat
More than one man
Takes a slap on the face
For breaking conversation
At the wrong time and place

Cross legged with one knee up high
This one might just be the guy
Let him do most of the talking
To prove he's got some place to go
Glance down when you get the chance
Yes, his imagination has gone to his pants
Keep your fingers on the straw
Tease your mouth into a smile
Raise those brown eyes when you swallow
Ain't no question where that boy will be
When the sun comes up tomorrow

She might decide one night was fine
She'll leave but stay within his mind
Like many a man who came before
Who cannot substitute the urge for more
Like the ghost that won't leave a house of pain
Without choice her image will remain
Fixed in folly of a sleepless dream
When they lie alone, awake at night
Smoking blue in the low light

She might decide to stay awhile
And strand herself upon his shores
She'll cook one meal and move right in
You'll find her clothes on every floor
Soon you can't seem to keep money saved
All your friends just roll their eyes
It's the lack of trust that wrecks you the most
Good parasites they won't suck you dry
Until they line up another host
Just when you think she's got to go
Lean and mean she lays you out
And ignites the savage in your soul
You live a dream three days long
Look around and she's gone
She left you bent, bruised and tight
Smoking blue in the low light

You're a fractured man, just like me
You want to dive deep to the other side
And drink the best of those memories
Yet from every shadow you run and hide
Creeping down sidewalks where her pony use to ride
Frozen by a picture outside a hairstyle boutique
Squint with suspicion at the smiling reflection
Cause you both know she's off in some other town
While you sit at home
To smoke and brood over what is right
She's throwing slag and cracking stone
Burning bright
Possessed in the white-hot, timeless origin
Of the low light

SALEM, MA

CAT ISLAND

Our love came rumbling with summer rain
Driven by restless southern winds
Bands of light tore apart the sky
Wide eyes, pupils alive, shining black
Heartbeat pounding as if being pursued
By a relentless predator
Knowing there is no escape
Only hope of inspired, evasive moves
To delay the wild instincts of our own lives
Fear and excitement fall together
A crescendo rises to rip leaves from trees
Until light and noise come together
Exploding the night, exposing everything
To pure, timeless anarchy

Thousands of years are stripped from our consciousness
Releasing shimmering echoes of innocence
Our senses return to untouched continents
Mechanical sounds are vulgar intrusions
Your breath is the force that pulls the tides
Your touch is the wind brushing over the sea
That sculptures the crest of each wave as it rides
The ocean receives us with violent disregard
Tossing in any direction, so sweetly at random
Alone on the sea, we share secrets never told
Drifting toward a dream that lovers rationalize
Finding the fears that we share surprise us the least
We tell stories that reflect the storm in our eyes
As we watch the front fade to the east

The emotions of nature do not quickly fade
This energy is rekindled beyond our limited range
Such passion sapiens can only wish to sustain
For after summer thunder passes
There is only summer rain

SALEM, MA

SHE CALLS

The telephone rings
I hear her voice
Strange chemicals are released
Heartbeat pounds my ribcage
I'm talking business
Trying hard to entertain
Say goodbye so slow
I'm swept by a tide that pulls only me
Tossed by the surf
Moved by her sea
All else is pushed aside by the flow
I want to know her,
Control her, submit to,
And to excite her
Just one look and I'd do anything
Give everything away
Except the unbound memory of her smile
And kind brown eyes

SALEM, MA

MAGICAL

Meeting by chance in the dark of the hall
She walked slowly past, then leaned on the wall
Gently we whispered of dawn coming soon
Such a vision that waited when I entered the room

What do you think? I made this all up
So fair a soul I could never corrupt
I swear to the sun, I swear to the sea
The woman I love, she came to me

I thought it was over, I was almost relieved
I know you will say it was all but a dream
This time I'm sure, I really do believe
Don't be annoyed if I should start to scream
She came to me
She came to me

What brings me back to want no other's touch?
So soon since last I lost myself in rhyme
Now I suppose I've said enough
Just let me tell you one last time
She came to me
She came to me

HARWICH, MA

ONLY ONE

When asked by a friend, "what is new?"
I fought with an urge to tell him the truth
The rush of my heartbeat nearly gave me away
Before I assured him all was the same

You see, the one I love gave me a sign
That begs me to believe she will soon be mine
Caution as my guide is losing its' sway
As I swell in her image and for her touch I pray

Like a willow in wind, wistfully I resist
Soon my roots relax, I free myself and follow
Discarding pagan possessions, none to be missed
What riches of the world could displace this sorrow?

Delivered by caravan from an ancient throne
Comes a gift of gold sent by Persian King
Tempered with red ruby, and sapphire stone
Yet cannot match the warmth one smile brings

No vision of this world could lift me higher
No temptation could shadow the flame of this fire
A visit from angels won't add to the surprise
Found in the glow of my true love's eyes

Now imagine the excitement of a single kiss
The brush of her lips across my face
To see her smile from so close as this
The smell of her hair, our silent embrace

A moment like this would bring out such pride
News of our romance I could never hide
I would ease through dark jungles
Climb the highest mahogany tree
I would beckon the eagles, challenge the sky
Gather fine pearls from the abyss in the sea
Breach the moonlight that mingles with mist
Encounter new species, delightful with envy
Return in a moment if it was your wish
Then spin off to a land where passions run free
To shout through the streets until all must believe
Where my heart now resides, it will always be

SALEM, MA

DUNES OF MONOMOY

Hey Donna

Can you see the dunes of Monomoy?
Rising to the east across the Sound
The horizon shimmers in the summer sun
We used to think the dunes were clouds
I could never forget the wonder
Of sitting with you on the beach
You'd offer to share your towel
I'd settle like a crab in the sand
My imagination sailed off to those dunes
To the west, I'd see the sun in your eyes

Hey Donna
Where does a love like this come from?
To change the orbit of boyhood dreams
So subtle at first as a change in wind
Until my heart hops like a petrel over the waves
A thousand paths that heart could follow
Only to strike the shoals after all these years
To find you smiling on the beach
Waiting on the towel that marks our place
With that same love now in reach
Forever to blossom when I see your face

R/V DELAWARE II, ATLANTIC OCEAN

DONNA B.

I fell in love with you
You'd seen enough of me
Not to stand below
When I was up a tree

I dug a hole so deep
Put my heart inside
Covered it up, so no one else would find
That I could only love you

A love as strong as this
It doesn't disappear
It can turn to spite
It can change to fear
Or smolder out of sight
For twenty-one years

I waited all this time for you
I waited all this time for you

If you fall in love with me
I've seen enough of you
To know the green of the tree
Goes fine with brown and blue

I waited all this time for you
I waited all this time for you
I waited for you.

GLOUCESTER, MA

SAMUEL JOSEPH

Welcome, Samuel
To our home on Portuguese Hill
High above, the endless sky winks and sparkles
Far away bombs are falling
No such worries for you here
You are innocent

Open your heart to the joy
Watch the trees give up their leaves
Crimson and gold
See the sun shine through the blind
Warmth and wonder
Hear your mother's voice
Sleep well and dream of love

GLOUCESTER, MA

BOOM BOOM BENJAMIN

Boom, boom, boom, boom
It's boom boom Benjanim

When he wakes up there's going to be trouble
When he wakes up there's going to be trouble

He's a chunky little guy
With a head so big
That it always hits first
Tumbling out of bed or over a toy

He's got big hands
That will pull you close
So he can pin you down
To scratch your face or bite your leg

Your brother's going to get you Benjamin
Your brother's going to get you Benjamin
It's boom boom Benjamin

He's a little love bug
Who gives the best hugs
Sometimes he gets so excited
He forgets to let go

Better not mess with Benjamin
Better not mess with Benjamin

Boom, boom, boom, boom
It's boom boom Benjanim

GLOUCESTER, MA

GRACE

In comes the blooming hyacinth
Dressed silken white for the cool of spring
Cultured well, every year to return
Unaware of the scent she'll bring

Out goes the blazing Halley's
With majestic tail cast from fiery core
The comet blooms but once for most
Then alights the heavens forevermore

Quiet grace and Irish eyes
Who could have chosen a better name?
Rising off this bed of stone
To return where from she came

HARWICH, MA

GALLOWAY

For every day there are two tides
For every man ten dogfish die
If one day one goes I know
I quench the teardrop in my eye

We toasted blood last time we met
I smelled the shroud in your sweat
You booted, you boozed, you were a mess
You were blood, now let blood rest

I hear the waves bash off this twisted coast
I fall in judgment before my reptile host
I smell the warm foul breath of the tortoise
Mixing in the pre-dawn mist of our Galapagos
Shading the moonbeam's path til I'm veiled in black
Settling to chill the sweat on my sun-burned back

From what depth did the serpent arise?
What force moved the dancing samurai?
Wild laughter bent to the charm of blow
My soul won't share a reason why

Now I wish that you were here
To explain to me your darkest fear
We'd express our love with easy excess
And slip from the shroud until another year

HARWICH, MA

MIDDLE BORN

From first born
To last born
No one could ever know
When the union of clans
Will churn out a saint
Or chip the halo
Leaving a hidden fracture
That will see the light of day
Despite the most elaborate canopies

Raised on a farm
A family of twelve
With natural joy and exuberance
Half-blooded Micmac grandmother
A cadence not heard 100 miles away
The middle born looked down the table
Saw laughter within the competition
And learned the gift would be giving

From first born
To last born
No one could ever know
The range of destiny
That could come from
The mixing of genes
The mother's abyss of love
The father's heavy hand
While shadows danced along the streets

Not raised to talk it over
To blame others or show strain
Late evening bickering
The random sputtering
Monkey grooming
Brushed back driving
All eased from the halo
Like steam rising off the ironing board

From first born
To last born
No one could ever know
How much she gave
Steadfast and unconditional
Giving of time and love
To those who had less
Now, this beautiful shining comet
Has slowly faded
A smile remains that crosses generations
The widow of one man
Who left this earth
Yet remains in her heart
Reminding her of this gift

HARWICH, MA

HAWKSNEST

The oaks are on the rise
The pines have had their time
First to claim the fields
Where the hickory were all cut down

Can I feel my past in these woods?
Will I join my ancestors in this dirt?
I feel something
Through the noise
When my dreams go deep
And the tide is behind me

Sleep well, Grandma
I measured your pulse as a child
You gave away the best you had
Calm and comfort
When anger would be so easy
Knowing where you are
Looking back to know you
Means the world to me

Rest free, Father
The dirt roads are gone
How did you absorb this change?
Carrying sins from before your birth
Of origin long lost to these grounds
To the mottled span of adaptation
And branches reaching for the sun
You gave to the future
To kin, friends, and strangers
A spirit released by the elements

HARWICH, MA

www.ingramcontent.com/pod-product-compliance
Lightning Source LLC
Chambersburg PA
CBHW031126080526
44587CB00011B/1127